STEAK AND CHERRY PIE

Mike Salazar

Copyright © 2015 Mike Salazar
All rights reserved
First Edition

PAGE PUBLISHING, INC.
New York, NY

First originally published by Page Publishing, Inc. 2015

ISBN 978-1-68213-481-8 (pbk)
ISBN 978-1-68213-482-5 (digital)

Printed in the United States of America

PASTOR MIKE'S TESTIMONY

Title: STEAK and CHERRY PIE
Purpose: To reveal the Power of God in a man's life
Objectives: To teach those that are incarcerated and on the street that

    God is Able to change any man
    From Crime to Christ,
    From Thug Life to His Life…

CHAPTER 1

EARLY DAYS (1960-1968)

"Okay, convict, take off your clothes. Now run your fingers through your hair, open your mouth, let me see behind your ears, turn around, and lift your left foot, right foot. Now bend over and spread 'em and cough…cough, cough!" Dang… first time that happens to you, it's embarrassing! So how did I end up in here? Check it out.

I still remember back in the days in Bakersfield when I was a kid. It was all about ditching school and shooting birds at the cemetery. I think I had a normal childhood for a Chicano kid. I mean besides being born in Oildale, a white power community back then, raised in an all-Mexican neighborhood next to Union Cemetery, and went to Potomac (Bessie Owens), an all-black school with a thousand black kids, maybe fifty Mexicans, and no white kids. It was pretty normal. What I mean is that I didn't grow up with cigarette burns on my body, or killing cats and dogs for fun, or pimping girls, or selling dope at seven or eight years old, or leader of the pack at nine.

Like I said, we lived next to the cemetery so all of us "at risk" kids used to play and roam around in there. I was real good in school—smart, disciplined, played the clarinet in the orchestra. Made first chair. Anyhow, school was cool until I hit the seventh grade. Then things began to change...

You know the scenario: poor ghetto child from a poverty-stricken, dysfunctional family (and I mean dysfunctional! Someday I'll tell you about it. By the way, *dysfunctional* means "damaged.") Anyway, I was twelve years old in Junior High School and hanging around with the fellas, getting drunk on a quart of beer, staying out late till 2–3 a.m. on the weekends, smoking cigarettes, and watching Captain Kangaroo.

I learned to smoke when I was ten. We used to go to the park after a baseball game and collect all the "vachas"(cig. butts) we could find and experimented. I started wearing khakis, town-craft T-shirts, Pendleton shirt (green), French toe shoes (black), stocking on my head at night to train my hair back with some pomade (*tu sabes*), and consciously training myself to walk like a Penguin and swagger with my knuckles almost hitting the ground. Learned all the hip and slang words like *Chale* (no), *Simon* (yes), *PorVida* (forever), *Rifa* (still don't know what that means), *Q-vo* (what's up ese).

Got into a neighborhood gang. Matter of fact, we created our own gang, Li'l Eastside.

The only thing was that we didn't jump ourselves in. Instead to prove ourselves we had to steal a trench coat and a derby hat and three pearls for the hat and shave our heads. Man, I don't know how I got away with stealing that trench but I did!

Matter of fact my *primo* (cousin) taught me how to steal funny books(comics) from the liquor stores when I was seven or eight years old. Never got caught. Stole a b-b gun and got busted coming out of the store by our neighborhood cop. He gave me a break. Learned to drive at twelve or thirteen years old by stealing cars. Joe, one of my friends, taught me how to hot wire a car. Stole over fifty cars (used to push them out of the driveway in the middle of the night, go for a ride, and take them back when we were done) Never got caught. But one time we almost got busted.

One night about 1 am, we were cruising over Mount Vernon Bridge when a cop saw us. He was going the other way, but he knew and we knew he knew. So Joe put the pedal to the metal and drove like he was a race car driver. He turned to the first dark street, slowed down, and told me to jump from a moving vehicle. We both jumped out and let the car run into a fence and hit a tree.

All the stunt man came out of me. I rolled and got up running for my life. You know how you get when you know the cops are right behind you. So I'm running like a bat out of hell! It's pitch black and I am running scared at full speed. I jump a fence and hit a clothes line at full speed. It caught my neck and dropped me. Needless to say, as I was lying there, I thought for sure I was busted, but we got away.

Which reminds me of another time when I hit something. I was at a party and the cops raided it. It must have been around midnight. So as I am running for my life again, running scared, I rushed full speed into an iron gate that I couldn't see. About knocked me out. I got away, but in the morning I realized that my nose was broken. Still broken to this day.

So without realizing which way my life was going (at that age I never thought about it), there I was on my way to being a career criminal. Caught my first case at twelve: malicious mischief (knocking down gravestones in Union Cemetery). Somebody gave us up (still don't know who told on us). One of the guys that got busted with me later on got killed in prison. After that, periodically I would get busted for small stuff like drunk, curfew violations, gang activity, go to juvenile hall for a few days—that was the routine for a while.

The worst part about that was that phone call from the cops to my mom: "Mrs. Salazar, we have your son here. You need to come pick him up." And there she goes in a taxi. Man, what a drag. I put my mom through some changes, but you don't think of those things when you're young.

My mom was a very dignified lady even though she was poor and lived in an old rundown house that was cold in the winter and hot in the summer. Everybody knew who my mom was in the neighborhood. She was the interpreter for all the Doña Julias (Spanish-speaking ladies). I remember that she always paid her bills. She used to read her Bible every day, but she didn't go to church. It used to bug me all the time when I got older. I'd say, "Mom, why do you read that book all the time? It don't do you no good! Look at your life and where you're at!" She'd say, "Someday you'll understand." Yeah right! What does my mom know…

CHAPTER 2

CAMP OWEN: CUT MY FINGERS OFF

Anyway, in the seventh and eighth grade I really began experimenting with drugs: Whites (uppers), Reds (downers), Yeska/Mota (weed), and Testors Glue. Glue sniffing really got out of hand. My whole neighborhood was sniffing. Matter of fact, every gang neighborhood was into that. We all used to go to Ben's Market because he was the only one that would sell to us by the box—twenty-four tubes! Everybody in the "hood" was always missing diapers and socks (used to roll it up and make a glue rag). Yeah, all my pant pockets were glued together. It got bad!

My face was getting all sucked up and had white spots starting to show. Man, I thought I looked good. (Reminds me of when I got out one time in the seventies. I was weighing 220 lbs, been lifting weights, and playing handball...*tu sabes* (you know what I mean), but I started using heroin from day one. About three weeks after I was out, I went to see my parole officer. I thought I was looking good. But my PO saw me and said, "My God, look what the cat dragged in. You look all sucked up!" (But I couldn't tell.) You never notice yourself when you're getting bad.

I graduated from the eighth grade (little did I know that that was the only diploma I would ever get). Now it's freshman time in high school. Went to BHS for about two months. Our crew got kicked out every three to four days for something or another or ditched school. Finally, I caught a case (arrested): "illegal brain cell deterioration"—glue sniffing.

My homeboy's dad busted us and there we go. Just turned fourteen years old in 1965 and sentenced to Camp Owen (county detention facility for juvenile delinquents). It was in the mountains. Never been to the mountains before except for once when I was about ten. The probation officer (who happened to be our uncle, who made sure that we never mentioned his name when we went to juvenile hall,) gathered all the little Mexican "at risk" juvenile delinquents from the hood and sent us to a Christian camp for a week. Only thing I remember is sleeping in a bunk house and singing around a camp fire "The Old Rugged Cross" that the camp guy taught us.

Yea, I'll always remember Camp Owen. I cut my fingers off in there and got two weeks added to my time for not following directions. They had just built a new wood shop (never been in one before). So the first time our class went in there, we acted like we knew what we were doing (I still think that I was still shaking off being "brain dead" from all that glue I sniffed). I turned on a jointer saw, and you can guess the rest. I didn't read the instructions and the instructor *never told us to turn on the machines*. He stepped out for a minute and said, "I'll be right back so don't touch anything." Naturally everybody turned on a machine.

So there I go again playing follow the leader (the story of my life so far). The saw smoothes wood, so I get a piece of wood about a foot and a half long and begin to slide it and push it through. Now what Mr. Brain Dead didn't know was that the instructions require a piece of wood at least two and a half feet long…duh! Too late. I was halfway through the cut when the wood started to shake in my hands. What do I do? Continue and hope the wood stops shaking?

STEAK & CHERRY PIE

Let go and let the wood hit somebody? I don't know. I didn't follow the instructions.

So I tried to push it through and *bam!* The wood slipped out of my hand and my fingertips were gone! There was so much blood I went into shock. Couldn't feel a thing. I just stood there, staring at my hand with my mouth open. My friend Joe (the car thief) saw what happened and started yelling, "Mr. Croker, Mike cut his fingers off!"

Cops took me to a "horse doctor" in Kernville. That old doc used bone clippers, or horse hoof clippers and I don't know what on my hand to trim the jagged bones. After he stitched me up and wrapped it up he said, "Son, you ain't never felt pain like you're gonna feel when those shots wear off. It's gonna hurt like the dickens!" (His actual words.) That was an understatement!

I got back to the camp and one of my friends came up to me with a glass jar in his hand and said, "Look, Mike, I saved your fingers [in small little pieces]." Now is that sick or what? We laughed about it later. Poor Homie, he's doing a life sentence for a murder. Been down since 1982. (Thirty-three years and recently got denied ten years until his next board hearing. I still keep in touch with him all these years.)

CHAPTER 3

CYA #74295

I finally got out. Man, what an experience in there. Only a fool would go back to a place like that que-no? (right?) Anyway, I'm out twenty-eight days and catch an armed robbery. What a joke! Three of us rob a taxi cab driver and got twenty-one dollars. Seven dollars for each of us. Plus, I took his (cabdriver) hat and lunch pail. (That's another story.) Anyhow, we got away and bragged about it to all our neighborhood.

Yup, within a week somebody told on the three of us and there we go again. I had just turned fifteen (1966) and on my way to YA (California Youth Authority). They sent us up north to NRGC (Northern Guidance Center). Met a lot of guys from San Jo (San

Jose), Watsonville, Frisco, etc. I remember that first night in the cell. It's funny how you can remember a certain song years later. That night, I was looking out my mesh screen window at the world beyond the barbed-wire fence and old Hank Williams came on singing "I'm so lonesome I could cry." The song fit! But I didn't cry because a man ain't supposed to cry que-no?

They shaved my head, fixed my teeth (ugly black fillings), gave me a psych evaluation, and went before the parole board with Miss DVI running it! Gave me ten months continuous at Paso (Paso Robles School for Boys). So there I go on my first bus ride with the State of California Department of Correction.

I'll always remember that bus ride. The cops chained a kid (about eight years old) to the wire mesh screen because he was acting like a kid. He was going to YA for two years. Anyhow, the guy that was chained next to me was a *veterano* (old guy early twenties) and he was going to DVI (Prison) for a murder beef. He began to give me some advice. He said, "Hey, youngster, if you're ever with a girl you care for and she goes out on you remember this...she's the one that gave it up, unless she was raped. Every dude, vato is like a dog just sniffing around and will try to have sex with her] but it's up to her to say yes or no. [Not exactly in those words.] So if it's worth killing for, don't kill the guy...kill the girl because if you just kill him, she'll still be with a *Sancho* [someone else] when you get busted."

That's what happened to him. He killed the dude instead of her and now he's going to the joint (prison) and she's with another guy! Now that's cold! Man, what a drag! It sounds like a soap opera. Anyway, he finished by saying, "Make sure you kill both of them if it's worth it to you, otherwise, turn around and walk away." So that was my lesson for the year. (What happened to the birds and bees advice for teens ? I still hadn't been with a girl yet.) Also, he tells me that if I am going to continue to commit crimes, I should not get any tattoos because that's the way most guys get identified and caught. (Never got any tattoos in prison. Just on the street)

CHAPTER 4

CYA PASO ROBLES SCHOOL FOR BOYS

I heard all the stories and listened to advice from whoever. But it didn't help none. I didn't know anybody. I admit I was scared. Oh well! It's time to put on my mask. I was thinking, "Whatever happens happens." Anyway, I remember making a deal with God (isn't that what everybody does?). I said, "God, if you help me make it through this so that I won't get no more time added, then I promise that I'll straighten up my act and quit drinking, getting high, and getting into trouble. I'll be a good boy." At that time, I really thought I meant it. I wanted to get out when I was supposed to. Sounded good, huh?

Yup, Paso Robles School for Boys was a school of "Hard Knocks." I was told before that I should mind my own business and do my own time—you know the old saying "you drink your whiskey and I'll drink my wine, you do your thing and I'll do mine." Sounded good, but it didn't work out that way. I was a *pescado* (a fish) and I had a lot to learn.

I learned how to pick locks and I learned that Mike really had a "dark side" that was hidden. You know, up until this time, I always thought of myself as a "regular" (just a normal kid gang member), a *vato* (homeboy). I tried to mind my own business, didn't go around picking fights, liked to party down, not fight, better to be a friend than an enemy, que no? Yeah, I was a *travieso* (always getting into trouble), committing crimes and getting high. That was me. But YA was another world with different rules.

First of all, I was alone in that institution. There were three other guys from Bakers (Bakersfield), all in different companies (dorms). We hardly ever saw each other. Right from jump street, I met some guys in my company (dorm) that made my life miserable. I tried to shine them on because I wanted to get out in ten months (classification had told me that if I messed up one time, they would transfer me). But I didn't realize that everyone thinks you're chicken if you're trying just to be "normal" and get out. Man, was I a "Tapaow, Square from Delaware."

Anyhow, things started happening behind my back (never to my face) until one day, me and my *camarada* (friend) from San Fer (San Fernando) were coming out of church with the rest of the companies (dorms). Note: Funny how you remember things, but the first time I ever saw a homosexual was at that church. He was a helper (altar boy). He got on the microphone and said, "Hotsy totsy, I'm a _____." It's funny the things you remember.

Anyway, a bunch of *vatos* (dudes) from a certain neighborhood (three lived in my dorm) were right behind us as we walked and, trying to be cute with their friends, called us a name (bad Mexican name). I blew it! I called 'em all out (challenge to fight), one on one or all together. It didn't matter to me. Forget the time, forget being a nice guy. I wanted to fight. As a matter of fact, I wanted to kill somebody, and I knew that I didn't need a weapon (if you know what I mean). Yup, I was *hot*! But you know what? Everyone backed down! (And I know I ain't no Rambo or Bruce Lee.)

They must have seen that look in my eye. So in order to save face, one of the tough guys from their group said, "I won't fight you but I'll fight your *camarada* (friend)." Now there's something wrong with this picture because this guy is my size. In 1966, I was about 5'10" and real skinny, and my partner was maybe five feet tall if he wore platform shoes. No way I'm gonna let that happen but my little partner said he would fight him.

I'm about to learn a big lesson in life (sometimes it's not the size of the dog that wins the fight, but the size of his heart —having heart goes along way). So there we go to the back of the dorm outside where all the fights take place. To myself I'm thinking, *Man, my little friend doesn't have a chance. He's too small!*

So I tell him that if he's getting beat up, just give me a sign and I'll jump in. (Pretty nice of me, huh?) Check this guy out. He knows he's too big for my friend so he's thinking that this is gonna be easy. So he shows off by taking off his coat real slow in a mocking kind of way, flexes his muscles, and says a few "do do" words, and they both square off.

Li'l homie goes at him and *baam!* Goliath tags him and knocks him down. Goliath was so confident that he lets him get back up. They square off again and *baam!* Down he went one more time. That's it! Gimme the sign. Enough is enough. I look at my friend but he shook his head no! Not yet! They square off again and *baam!* Down he went for the third time. That's it, man. Gimme the sign… gimme the sign!

But when he looked up at me, I saw that look. His eyes said it all. I didn't even ask. He got up and charged Goliath and tackled him down and beat him down soooo bad that it was embarrassing. I pulled out that little pipe I had stashed and threatened everybody in that circle, yelling like a mad man (too much adrenaline pumping I think).

Anyway, after that, nobody ever bothered us again. Yeah, me and li'l homie made life miserable for those guys in our dorm until they went home. We were *gacho* (mean) to them but they had that coming. Moral of the story? One, don't start something you can't finish. Two, what comes around goes around. Three, don't stir up the monster.

Funny thing but years later in prison, after I got saved in there (more on that story later) that guy that got beat down "drove up" to the yard and I apologized to him for all that "madness" in YA. He looked at me like I was crazy. Oh well, I tried. As a matter of fact, if I offend anyone reading this book, *despensa*…apologies. My purpose for writing this book is so that you might give God a chance to prove Himself to you. So with that hope in mind, I have chosen to be as real and transparent as I can.

CHAPTER 5

GETTING OUT AGAIN

I finally got out of Paso. Man, what a feeling when you get released. Nothing like it! Someone told me not to look back because it was bad luck and that I would be back. But as we were leaving the institution, I looked back. At the bus station, somehow I remembered the promise I made to God. I did get out without doing more time. He kept His end of the deal but I didn't keep mine(me and a couple of other parolees got drunk at the bus station). Anyway, from that day on, I made up my mind never to ask God like that again because I knew I couldn't follow through. I couldn't keep my promise to Him.

Yeah, I hit the streets and didn't last too long. I started drinking, smoking weed, and committing crimes again. I was a youngster and still learning about the streets, about life, and about people.

One day, me, Weasel, and a couple of other homeboys broke into Rainbow Market (neighborhood store). We stole beer, cigarettes, and the usual junk food. Filled up three big tubs. Got away clean. Then one day at school (miracle I was on the campus that day) I was called into the office and two detectives were waiting for me. *Baam!* Handcuffed! There I go to the police station and there goes my high school education.

When I got there, Weasel is sitting there handcuffed. When the cops split, he tells me "Man, you're a cold dude for snitchin' on me." I said, "What are you talking about? I didn't tell nobody nothing." He says, "Yeah right, the cop told me it was you." (Does this scenario sound familiar if you're reading this book?) I told him, "Hey, they picked you up first homeboy, not me!" "You're the one that said something!" Anyway, he said he didn't tell either. So who did? It couldn't be our hero, could it? The OG gangster we looked up to? The other guy involved in the crime? No way! Uh-uh! (Street Lesson # 7 Yup, he told on us.)

CHAPTER 6

MERRY-GO-ROUND

Well, here I go again! Got told on again. Went back to YA on a new case, a 459 Burglary. What a drag! They sent me back to Paso Robles. Did about seven to eight months. Easy time! The only thing I remember about then was a homeboy escaped and almost drowned in the river. (That boy did a lot of time over the years, got involved in a prison gang, but today, he's doing good serving the Lord.)

Anyway I get out. Don't remember too much again. Dead brain cells again I think.

Getting high on whatever's around. But I wasn't out too long when David picked me up to go swimming. It was night time and it was Bakersfield Hot! We went to a rich part of town where his cousin lived. The house on the corner had a pool, so we jumped the fence to go swimming. (It's funny because after a while you don't even think about consequences.) So there we are in our "crime fighters" (tantarans, skivvy shorts). Can't remember if we wore boxers back then. Swimming like we owned the place.

After a while, David has a bright idea. Let's break in! Well, you know the story. Mr. Brain Dead can't say no because he's a follower, so there we go. The blind leading the blind. We bust a window (might as well have woke up the whole neighborhood), climbed in, and start going through everything in that house. I hand him the stuff and he takes it to the car, back and forth…back and forth. Now this is *dumb*! We get hungry, so we start making something to eat—eggs and ham with all the trimmings(yeah, it was good).

All of a sudden the cops show up (you think?). We run through the house and out the front door. *Boom!* A shotgun goes off and hits the side of the house. Oops! Excuse me, but I'm going back in the pad (house). David decides to make a run for it through the back yard. I'm running thru the house as he's running through the yard and I'm yelling, "Run, Forrest, Run" (joke). Truthfully I said, "Go, David, go!" Just as he's jumping over that wooden fence, *boom!* Shotgun knocks the whole fence down. I'm thinking, "Man, he's dead." Just at that moment I hear the cops with a police dog at the front door. So I try to hide up in a closet. I overhear them saying, "I know there's one more in the house. Go get him, Killer. Tear him to pieces." (Who let the dogs out…woof! woof!). Talk about scared! I yelled out, "Here I am. I give up."(Courage just went out the window.) So there I go to juvenile hall in my crime fighters. How embarrassing! Well, you guessed it. There I go back to YA again. (Man, this is getting ridiculous)

CHAPTER 7

MT. BULLION FORESTRY CAMP

This time they sent me to Mt. Bullion Forestry Camp in Mariposa, California. Me and another kid were the youngest ones in that camp. So two things I remember—forest fire and peanut butter.

Ever been to a forest fire? I was in the camp two days with no training when we get called to a fire. Drove all night in an army truck. Still remember that name "Kanaki Gulch fire." We turned a comer and there it was, three mountains on fire and painted orange red. We hiked up that mountain, ten feet apart. Talk about out of shape. I've been smoking steady since I was twelve. Anyway, with tongues hanging out we made it to the top. Cops split us up, two guys every hundred yards. Our mission? Make sure the fire doesn't get past us and don't let the snakes, bears, mountain lions, or any other poisonous animal or insect attack you. Anyone caught sleeping gets thirty days added to his time and you won't get paid your fifty cents a day! Man oh man! What is a poor boy gonna do? Yup! We fell asleep! Woke up in the morning with the cop standing over us shaking his head. He gave us a break. After that fire, I knew that I was not cut out to be a fire fighter. End of story!

Back at the camp the routine was cutting brush every day. Now this older guy David, he was from LA, tells me, "If you smell peanut butter let me know." Peanut butter?

So one day when we were out cutting brush I smelled peanut butter. I told David and he found a plant with pods hanging on the branches. Loco Weed! (Jimsonweed). It's supposed to be some kind of psychedelic high, whatever that is! This is 1967. I just turned seventeen and never heard of LSD yet. Anyway, he took the whole plant back to the barracks, cut it all up, and put it in a milk shake. Naturally he tried to talk us into doing it with him. Mr. Brain Dead finally said no. Thank God! But he ate the whole thing.

So there we are, sitting on our bunks staring at him, waiting for something to happen. And it did. That loco weed hit him and he started acting crazy. He started walking down the dorm when his pants fell down to his ankles. He kept on walking right in front of the officer. He was oblivious. He entered the mystical La La Land. And ended up in the psych ward for two weeks. I will definitely not try that stuff. I ain't that stupid. (Yet later on I smoked Dummy Dust PCP. So what's the difference? Duh!)

Oh well. I finally got out in 1968. I'd be turning eighteen pretty soon. I haven't accomplished a thing. I lost all my teenage years. Never had the guts to finish school. Instead I followed my friends. [Thinking back on my life as a teen, I remember that I tested high scholastically and had all college prep classes as a freshman. But I had no one to encourage me to finish school or tell me, "You can do it, Mike. Don't be a dummy. You're smart. Don't hang around with all the zeros and two's." (Schools used to grade the levels of intelligence through your test scores 0, 1, 2, 3, 4. Three being average and 4 being college prep or above average.) I was a level 4 but all the "cool" people were zeros and two's. The "influence" they had was too strong for this easily influenced Chicano kid so I naturally gravitated to my "special ed" friends. Oh well. Wish I could've walked across that stage to get my high school diploma with everyone yelling when they called my name. I wish I could've went to my high school prom. I wish…I wish…Shoulda…coulda…woulda is too late. I made my choice. Bad choice but still my decision. Next chapter!

CHAPTER 8

STREET LIFE (1968-1972)

How long will you go on being a fool?

—Proverbs 1:22 (TLB)

1968...Vietnam and the draft...out on parole. My parole officer gave me three choices: go to Vietnam, get married, or go back to prison (this time as an adult). Not much of a choice, huh? I didn't want to go back to CYA or to prison. I wasn't very patriotic, but my girlfriend was pregnant. So I did the honorable and right thing and got married. I'm eighteen years old, got a wife and a new baby, and no education. Now what? Get a job.

So I get a job at Travette Mfg. Co. at $1.65 an hour. (First job in my life, man, what a career.) But I was legal and actually living the American dream (the cops weren't chasing me). My mom was happy, my parole officer was happy, my wife was happy. Everybody was happy except me! Why? Because I was going nowhere fast! Too many bills and not enough money!

In 1969, in my mind, I have a Mickey Mouse (lousy) job roofing campers, going nowhere fast. So, I started slingin' dope (slang for pushing, dealing, selling, trafficking in narcotics, etc.) Nowadays, everybody's selling dope. Mexican gangs, black gangs, Asian gangs, white gangs, police officers, grandmas, truckers, correctional officers, mayors, movie stars, Wall Street brokers, and regular old John Q. citizens. Maybe your next-door neighbor, who knows? Or if you know how to work the system, you can sell weed (pot) at a medical marijuana facility legally and make a lot of money because everybody's trying to go get their "Pot Card" nowadays.

Anyhow, I sold whatever I could get my hands on —weed, pills (especially "fender benders" or "gorilla pills," Red Devils, downers) hash, whatever. Then one day, I met my first long-haired hippie at work. He was kind of strange. Always talking about the "cosmos" and Timothy Leary…turn on…tune in…drop out (whatever that means). Well, he turned me on to two hits of Mescaline (synthetic peyote). What the heck is that? No Mexican has ever heard of that before. Needless to say Mr. Hippie told me it was like strong weed. Yeah right!

I'll always remember that first psychedelic trip. I became one with the universe (whatever that means) and hallucinated all night. The hippie became my connection. I think I was one of the first "low rider hippie connections" in Bakersfield. Note: One of the dangers in experimenting with drugs is that you might try something that you'll really like and then you're in trouble!

Needless to say, I got off CYA parole and like I said, "living the American Dream" (not being chased by the cops). But my marriage didn't work. I think I was too young. Anyhow, she took the baby and went to LA. I stayed and really got into selling dope. I sold anything I could get my hands on—jars of Reds (Downers) and Whites (Uppers) (jar is a thousand pills), kilos of weed, hundred hit bags of Mescaline and LSD. (They used to call me Mescaline Mike.)

CHAPTER 9

PRISON FLASHBACK

SAN QUENTIN

Always remember years later when I ended up in San Quentin Prison.
    We just came down from a riot in Susanville Prison and were told by an officer when we were in North Block that we were going to get "hit" (killed) as soon as we got to the yard. Man, I ain't gonna lie. I was scared but I didn't show it. (You know, got to put on

the mask). I didn't think that I knew anybody in SQ, so all of us that went to the main line agreed to watch each other's back. Anyway, talk about scary. First day in North Block, they let us go down from the fifth tier to take a shower and a "cannon" went off. That's what it sounds like when the guards open fire inside a block.(Two guys were killing each other downstairs) Oh well, just another day at "Baghdad by the Bay"(SQ).

The day they let us out on the upper yard it was packed with convicts. As I'm walking, I didn't recognize anybody. All of a sudden I hear someone say "Mescaline Mike!" There's Johnny B. (one of my first white boy friends). Actually, first time I went to CYA it was two Mexicans and two white boys in the back seat of a sheriff's car. (He was one of them) He was a sight for sore eyes. Man, was I glad to see him. Why? He was a plumber on the yard and had access to weapons. Just telling the truth. Anyway, we reminisced for a while about old times. Especially when I gave him a "hit" of mescaline and he ran butt naked down Baker St. Man, what a laugh! Poor Johnny. Spent most of his life in and out of institutions "for higher learning" starting at eight years old—Frico, Nellis, Paso, Preston, etc. Ended up killing a guy at a bar when he got out the last time. Johnny's not too big so when he was insulted by "Goliath," he went home and got his gun and shot the guy six times. End of story.

CHAPTER 10

TIJUANA, MEXICO

Anyhow, as I was saying, I was selling everything. Always trying to meet the right "connections." Drug trafficking became my career. I think it was 1969 or 1970 when I got involved with Pancho and his gang. (He was the first "big time" pusher I hooked up with…May the Lord have mercy on him. He passed away quite a few years ago.) Pancho and associates made a killing in 1968 during "Operation Intercept." That was when Customs stopped every car at the S. D. border and checked for drugs, which reminds me of the first time I went to TJ—Tijuana, Mexico.

Me, Vince, and Stella crossed the border high on acid. We went bar hopping all night. No real age limit over there. (I was maybe nineteen years old.) Anyway, Vince took off with a cab driver and came back with a kilo of marijuana. He bought it for $25. It was the size of a large brick. So he has a great idea. Let's smuggle it across the border. I should've said no but I didn't. Well, we decided to put the kilo in the carburetor breather. It fit perfect and there we go. But instead of waiting till the morning when all the traffic lined up, we tried crossing about three in the morning, hardly any cars in line at all. Major mistake!

So there we are, the Three Stooges in line waiting for the customs officer to approach our car. Naturally I'm driving. So when we pulled up to the custom station, the officer comes to the window and asks, "Where are you from?" I tell him, "The good old USA, sir." He can tell from our accent that we are not from Mexico.

"What were you doing in TJ?"

"We just came to party, sir."

I was very respectful. I'm sure he believed us. So he just did his normal routine, looked around and asked me to pop the trunk. Well, guess what? Vince forgot that he had a pound scale in the trunk.

So when the officer saw it, he gets suspicious and puts a tag on the window and directs us to drive to the secondary—the shakedown area! Dang, we are busted! Vince panics and tells me to make a run for it in the car. Yeah right! How far do you think we're going to get? You run. I'm sticking this out till the hubcaps fall off. So the inspection officer comes out of the office, comes to our car, pops the hood, and opens the breather on the carburetor, and bam, pulls out his gun and places us under arrest.

What we didn't know was that that's the first place a customs officer looks to see if you're smuggling something. Duh! Too late. It's all about at least five years in the federal penitentiary for smuggling. So there we go with our hands up in the air heading to the customs office.

Once there, they strip search us as they tear up the car searching for more drugs.

Well, we sat there all night till about ten in the morning just waiting. Finally, a couple of officers call us to the counter. Our IDs were laying there. He told us, "Get your IDs and get the hell out of here!" I looked at him as if he was crazy or something. I said, "You're letting us go?" He said, "Yup, because you guys got burned. That was a kilo of alfalfa. If we had found one seed of pot in your car, we could have arrested you. But we didn't. Now get the—out of here!"

Man, I couldn't believe it. We got burned. No, I take that back. Vince got burned from a cab driver that sold him a kilo of alfalfa. Now what are the odds on that? Needless to say, that was the first time that I was glad to be burned!

CHAPTER 11

DRUG SMUGGLER

Anyway, back to the story. Everything, especially Pot, was nowhere to be found in Bakersfield because of Operation Intercept. During that time I remember thinking, "Whoever is the first one to bring in 'weed' is gonna get rich!" Well, it was Pancho. All the kilos of marijuana that we sold smelled like gas. (They were being smuggled in gas tanks.) Note: I can talk about that now because that method of smuggling is so old, nobody does it like that anymore.

But let me talk about smuggling again because that is a hot topic in the United States right now. Back in the eighties, when I was in a backslidden condition or I could say I relapsed and went back to my old ways, (I'll talk about that later), I ended up getting involved with one of the *familias* or *cartels* from Mexico. My *primo* (cousin) Gilbert was a "big time" dealer back in those days and I worked for him and his crew as a *pistolero* (body guard).

I basically "got volunteered" to ride shotgun with a pilot. My job was to make sure the "load" got to the destination safely. Anyway I was supposed to get $5,000 a load. So it sounded good but I really didn't know what I was getting myself into. Smuggling drugs from Mexico is not like the old "Miami Vice" TV program. Nope. It's a whole lot different. Once the deal was made with the pilot, me and his co-pilot had to go check out the landing strip in Baja California, to make sure the runway was good.

The co-pilot was a Vietnam veteran helicopter door-gunner. The average life expectancy of a door-gunner during the Vietnam days was ten days. Man, you had to be a little crazy to do that and he was. He was a big ol' peckerwood. He told me he used to put the head phones on, play Jimi Hendrix, and start blasting anything that moved. He did two tours. Crazy dude.

So we get to our destination. A small town called Portovino that had one hotel. When we get there, I wanted to make a phone call and was told that I had to drive 125 miles to use the phone. No such thing as cell phones back then. The next morning someone was supposed to contact us at that hotel. That's all I knew.

The next morning as we were eating breakfast, a short little Mexican dude comes to our table and says to me, "Tokayo?" That was my nickname to the gang from Mexico. I said yes and he told us to go with him. So we get in the back seat of this car and Manolo turns around and introduces himself with his badge. Policía Judicial Federal de Mexico—federal police—the feds. Mr. Door-Gunner about peed in his pants. The driver's name was Chepo. Little did I know that those two guys were some major players with one of the five crime families that used to run Mexico. Anyway, Manolo laughed and said not to worry because they worked for the "Mero Mero," (Big Crime Boss) and that they were taking us to the air strip. (Got to admit, that was a little scary.)

Make a long story short, everything was cool and we went back to Orange County. So me and Charlie the pilot took off from an airfield in a big Cessna six-seater. Charlie used to be a Korean war pilot but now a professional smuggler.

I had never been in a small plane before so you can imagine the thoughts going through my head. That plane had two steering wheels, two sets of pedals, etc. So I asked him, "What should I do if you have a heart attack?" He said, "You're going to die." No ifs, ands, or buts about it. There are no parachutes, and even if there were, it wouldn't do no good because we were flying too low and I would hit the ground before it opened up. Man, that was comforting!

So we finally get to the air strip, a dry salt lake bed. Before we land, he tells me that the safest place when we hit the ground is on the plane because if anything happens, he's taking off. (Manolo had told us that everyone was paid off...police, Feds, but not the army.) That's all we need is an army patrol showing up. (My job when we hit the ground was to pump fuel in the wings while the ground crew loaded up the plane with bales of drugs.) Needless to say, we flew out of there without a gunfight. (Man, was I glad to be in the air.)

Anyway, we flew low across the border to the Mojave Desert where my primo Louie was waiting with his crew in a ravine. When I tried contacting him on the walkie-talkie, I heard NASA talking to the *Discovery* space shuttle as they apparently were entering Earth's atmosphere. Then a couple of F-15 jets passed us by. I just waved like an idiot! Well, we landed, dumped all the bales out, and took off again. Man, that was a long day.

Then we repeated everything the next day. So on the next day when we landed in Mexico, Manolo told me in Spanish to stay with them so they could load two hundred more pounds where I was sitting. What could I say? I wanted to say heck no, I ain't staying back to get in a gunfight with the Mex. army and get captured and tortured and end up in a Mex prison! Because that's what really happens to everyone when you get caught. But what I said was *horale* (okay)! Couldn't be chicken now. Charlie looked at me and said, "They want you to stay, huh? See you later!"

And there goes my ride flying off into the sunset. Manolo gives me an AR-15 and a Colt 45 and tells me to follow them up the mountain trail and if the army shows up to stay close because they have an escape route. (Wish I was on that plane.)

We stood at their hiding place for a couple of days. A guy on a donkey would bring us breakfast every morning. At night, I taught them how to "shoot craps," American rules. (Always carried a pair of dice with me during those days). Well, I took all their money even though I tried to lose because I was taking a chance that they would get mad and we get in a gunfight. But they were cool about it. Oh well, the end of this story is that I made it back to San Diego in one piece. (Actually I had asked God to do me a favor even though I didn't deserve it. I asked Him that if things went wrong and I got busted (arrested), to please let me get busted on the American side. And I wasn't joking!)

CHAPTER 12

"ALL ABOUT THE MONEY"

OK, one day, I'll finish telling this story. But just to summarize it, the load got ripped off (hijacked), me and Louie got it back, then I got burned, then a couple of months later, Manolo and Chepo [Guadalajara Cartel] show up at my door in OC and asked me if I wanted to "go to work for them." Man, I was broke so naturally I said yes. (And what happened next is another story.) Note: The fact that I didn't get paid and was "broke" was the result of other people's greed. That's the reality of the "dope game." From the street hustler to the main connections, that's the way it is. You never have enough money. More is never enough. So when greed sets in, people will get down and dirty and do whatever it takes to get that money even if it means robbing your friends and family or even your own gang. Some will even turn you in to the police or set you up to get robbed or killed.

Eventually, someone will find out what you have done or get tired of what you are doing and you'll end up dead or in prison and might end up in an "SNY" (sensitive needs yard) or better known as PC (protective custody). And that's a fact of life.

Like I said, I got burned and was broke. So for a couple of months there, me and my old friend Bobby G. were driving from OC to Beverly Hills every day to work setting tile. Bobby G. was a bank robber/dope fiend. He and his ex-wife used to rob banks. As a matter of fact, a few years later he got arrested for a bank robbery and escaped from the brand-new metropolitan federal detention center in downtown Los Angeles from the top of an eight-story building. Might as well been a movie. Story came out on *LA Times*. Tied a bunch of sheets together and climbed out through a hole they cut in a wire mesh screen roof. Five of them escaped and slid down eight stories and got away. (The next day he shows up at my house in Palm Springs, but that's another story.)

Bobby G. did about twenty years for that bank robbery. Today, he's off parole and clean.

CHAPTER 13

EXPERIMENTING

Anyway, back to 1969 to 1970. Yup! It was on. I was buying and selling weed, pills, mescaline, acid, whatever! Nickle and dime at first but then on to bigger and greater things. Later in life I read something that made sense to me: "There is a way, a path, a road that seems right to a man, but the end of that road is the way of death or the end of that road is always a dead end." But when you're young and dumb, you don't know that yet!

One day, Pancho called a meeting. He said that all pill and weed transactions were going to stop because they were too bulky. From now on, it was all about "Chiva…Carga…Negra…*heroin*! My first remark was "can you make any money from that?"

Well duh! But I didn't know any *Tecatos* (heroin addicts) except for the one that gave me my first shot. We worked together on my first "slave job" in 1968. We roofed campers together. In 1968, (eighteen years old) up until that time, I had never stuck a needle in my arm. I never liked needles. But ask any addict what they said when they were young. "I'll never fix" (inject). I'm not that stupid!

Well, we all said that and meant it for a while. *But*, we didn't know or understand that drinking beer, smoking weed, dropping pills, doing acid, snorting something up our nose, or smoking the pipe (experimenting) would more than likely lead to "mainlining," injecting yourself with an *erre* (syringe). Most of the old addicts I used to know and the ones I know today started drinking and smoking weed first. Experimenting with whatever was around, before they ever considered sticking a needle in their arm.

Today, so many people young and old are "shooting up" Meth. Sad. The life of an addict is a horrible life to say the least. Addiction can turn a good boy into a monster and a young girl into a whore. (More about that later.)

I'm not sure why I "fixed" (injected) that first time. But every payday Chava would tell me, "Come on, youngster, let's go fix." I always said no! But one day I said yes. (I was eighteen.) A nickel bag almost killed me. I was sick for two days. Didn't like it and didn't touch it again for almost a year. I tried it again, (nineteen years old) just a little bit, and I liked it. But I didn't do it again for a while.

CHAPTER 14

MR. BIG STUFF

It's 1970, Pancho and the crew were making big money. They had the whole valley "sewed up" selling heroin. But I wasn't making any money. I didn't know any tecatos (heroin addicts) in Bakesfield. So Pancho sent me up north with two ounces of pure heroin. The rest is history.

I made so much money in San Jose ($2,000 a day, selling $15 dollar bags) I actually didn't know what to do with it. (That was a lot of feria [$$] for a young pup.) I was twenty years old, bought a brand-new Fiat convertible, had an apartment furnished with the best, night clubbing, you know the story. Thought I was Pimpin Will from Sugar Hill, never worked and never will, get your hand shook and your money took…yeah, yeah, yeah, Mr. Big Stuff, who do you think you are!

Making runs back and forth to Bakersfield, pick up, distribute, pick up, distribute —that's the dope game. But one day I happened to call my mom on the phone from San Jose. She tells me that there was a big drug raid and 137 people got busted.

I knew most of them and Pancho was one of them. I call him up and he tells me to lay low. They were out on bail and more indictments were coming out. The newspaper even named the informant. I couldn't believe it. I sold to that dude twice in the last year. I *knew* I'm busted. So I tell my mom not to tell anybody anything if someone comes looking for me (especially the cops).

(My mom was cool sometimes. One day, years later when I was on parole, I was in the bedroom, in my mom's house, bagging up some heroin. Just like that, the parole officer is at the front gate. Man, I panicked. I go outside hoping he doesn't come in to search. He leaves, I go back inside, and the plate of dope is gone. My mom said she flushed it down the toilet because she didn't want me to get busted. I almost cried. Man, now I'm in the hole, I owe, I owe, I owe. I went on and on for about ten minutes when mom came out with the plate—she was just teaching me a lesson.)

My mom would always "cover for me" (not say anything) and was always trying to teach me a lesson but I usually never paid attention. She always used to tell me, "Dime con quien andas, y te digo quien eres" (tell me who you run around with and I'll tell you who you are or who you'll be like). Naturally, she was right.

Anyway, I had to lay low for a while. That was all right. I'm twenty years old, I had an apartment, a car, about $30,000 saved up, and two ounces of heroin left. So I figured I'd just wait until things started rolling again. (Sometimes things don't work out like you planned,) Make a long story short I got bored waiting around.

CHAPTER 15

ADDICTED AND DIDN'T KNOW IT

One day, this friend of mine came over with a "rig" (syringe, cooker, *panio* [handkerchief]). So me, him, and two girls that never fixed before did a little taste. Well, the next day we did it again and again for the next three weeks…every day.

One day I said to myself, "I'm tired of shooting heroin. I'm going back to Bakersfield." So I took off kinda late and ended up in a motel room in Los Banos, California. The next morning I woke up sicker than a dog! I had the flu, pneumonia, and felt like I was on a medieval torture rack all at the same time. (My bones ached bad.)

Believe it or not, I didn't know what was wrong with me. I really thought I had a bad case of the flu. You see, nobody ever told me about being hooked or addicted. I sold to addicts but I never really understood what they were going through. I didn't care about all that anyway. It was always about the money. Always has been about the money. (That old saying is true, "The love of money is the root of all evil.")

So there I go back to San Jo (San Jose). When I get to my apartment, guess who was waiting for me? Yup! The other three. I tell my friends "I got the flu." He said, "Flu! You ain't got no flu. You're dope sick just like us. Do a little and see what happens." I did and I was miraculously cured. (Being sarcastic.)

That was the first time I was ever addicted and realized that I was. (Here comes the dominoe effect) Everything went downhill fast after that! I went on a two-year run fixing every day.

Lost everything, sold everything, and became a statistic…a junkie, a dope fiend, a tecato, a bum, a liar, cheat and thief, a manipulator, con man, and a user! I turned into a no-good, low-life, riffraff, park bench, box car, gutter-sleeping, nose-picking, feet-smelling, nickel-and-dime dope fiend. To say the least.

CHAPTER 16

SOMETHING TO THINK ABOUT

But I can't blame nobody. The decisions I made early in my life came back to haunt me. It took me a long time to understand that. I used to blame everyone, as I got older, for me being an addict and a convict for all those years. Bottom line was that I made some bad, stupid choices in my life.

Yes, I was a poor ghetto child, raised in a dilapidated neighborhood, with dysfunctional parents and family members. Never had hugs and kisses. Easily influenced. A follower. Could never say no. A product of my environment (if you're a sociologist), criminally minded (if you're a psychologist), criminally bent with genetic criminal genes (if you're a DNA scientist), or maybe I was just born to be a dope fiend and in prison all my life (if you believe in fate). Whatever! It was still my choice!

They say addiction is a disease. I guess you can look at it that way. But once all the "dope fiends" found out that they had a disease, they all applied for SSI to get the money. Steady income. Dope fiend dream come true. Big joke!

The government finally wised up and stopped giving SSI money for drug addiction. Now you have to have a "dual diagnosis"—an addiction with a mental disorder. Guess what? Drug addicts are smart. They figured out what to tell the doctors in order to be classified with a dual diagnosis. Anyway, I thought I'd throw that in. Remember, that's just my opinion, so let me be fair. There are people that really have that condition, but a lot don't. Next page!

CHAPTER 17

THE SEVENTIES, ANGEL DUST, AND HEROIN

From 1970 to 1980 was a time for me, personally, to experience the reality of hard-core heroin addiction, living in a cage with other animals (prison) and the politics of prison gangs.

During 1970 to 1980, "Angel Dust" (PCP) and heroin were the topic of the day. I knew the guys that were bringing in PCP into Bakers (Bakersfield). That stuff is dangerous. I knew three persons that died smoking that. Two were dealers that smoked it and one was a girl we all knew that hung herself in her garage in front of her two kids. That was bad.

The other two were just as tragic. One died in four feet of water while he was swimming. How? He thought down was up and up was down. You lose your equilibrium on PCP. Also, you act strange. This same guy got busted, just before he died, sitting butt naked with only his sweater on in his neighbor's house. I think that's strange, que no? The other guy used to sell heroin as well as Angel Dust. (Note: I wonder who named it "Angel" Dust. More like "devil dust.")

Anyway I go to his pad to cop (buy). When I walked in, I saw a few guys sitting on the couch, a long table with stacks of money on it and homeboy twirling a gold-plated 357. magnum with an eight-inch barrel in his hand. He tells me, "Hey Mike, you got *huevos* [guts]?" He was all smoked out of his head and wanted me to play "Russian Roulette" with him. One bullet in the chamber, spin it, put it to your head, and pull the trigger. I said, "I got guts but I ain't stupid. Just give me the dope I came for and I'm out of here." He said, "Come back in ten minutes."

So I took off and came back in ten minutes. I should have known something was wrong—no cars in the driveway and front door wide open. But when you're dope sick you're not thinking. I walk in, take a peek, guys and money are gone and homeboy's dead. End of story!

It was bad back then. Everybody was smoking that junk. I tried it a few times. Especially if I was dope sick. It used to knock me out. One time I went to this night club. In the parking lot, a friend of mine gave me a hit of a "super kool," a dipper, something new on the street. So me like a "dummy" take two big hits off this Kool cigarette. I told him thanks and walked off. I got to the entrance of the club and froze. People walking past me, looking at me strange, but I can't talk or move. The bouncer comes up to me and says, "What's wrong with you, Mike"? I just look at him all stupid. I just mumble something. He said, "You took a hit off that junk, huh?" I sounded like Frankenstein answering him. Needless to say, that's the last time I tried that stuff.

Talking about PCP reminds me of my "cellie" in Soledad prison in the eighties. He was a PCP cook (a barrio chemist). Just like the meth lab cooks. He explained the whole process and the chemicals used in the manufacture of PCP. Who in the world could invent something like that? Had to be the devil. Ugly drug. He was a youngster with a murder beef. I used to cap on him because he hardly had any hair. He said when he was in the LA County Jail for two years fighting that murder, he used to wake up with patches of hair on his pillow. I guess you could say he was stressed out?

Anyway, twenty-five years later I happened to run into him at one of the prisons that I go to nowadays to minister. It was good seeing him but sad that he has never gotten out. So many men that I have talked to or know personally that are doing life sentences help me to remember what the grace of God in my life really means.

I try to explain that to those that I talk to, especially the youngsters. One of the saddest experiences that I've encountered was when I used to go to Tehachapi prison and talk to the youth with life sentences (YOP program). These kids are sixteen and seventeen years old with life sentences because they got tried as an adult for a crime they committed. They were from all over California and had to be warehoused, segregated until they turned eighteen because they were minors.

When I would look out to the twenty or thirty kids that would come out to one of my church services, I could see myself in them when I was a kid. Man, they were too young. What a waste of young lives. That is one of the reasons that I keep going back to the institutions. Maybe I can make a difference in someone's life regardless of their circumstance.

CHAPTER 18

CRC (CALIFORNIA REHABILITATION CENTER)

California
AUGUST 7, 1974 Twenty-Three Years Old

So at the end of 1972, I got busted for Poss. For Sale and a weapons charge (sawed-off shogun). Sentenced to CRC (Civil Addict Program) on a suspended sentence of five to fifteen years. That's the way they did it back then in CRC (California Rehabilitation Center) a Civil Addict Program.

Over two thousand addicts from all over California in the same place. A state-run program trying to "cure" us dope fiends. That was a joke. Just like the word "rehabilitation." All a joke.

I remember dorm 10 was a therapy dorm. "Attack Therapy" was used as well as every other kind of weird psychological deprogramming methods. It was voluntary so you know we never went there! Excuse me! I was in dorm 16 in the "hotel." That's where they housed dual commitments A#, B#, and us N# that are exclusionary material (means we really shouldn't be there because of the seriousness of our charges).

Met a lot of guys there from both sides of California. Black, brown, and white. I remember I met this white boy, who became a friend of mine over the years. They called him the Rodeo Drive gangster or the Beverly Hills Hustler, something like that. (His family was rich and so he was born with a silver spoon in his mouth so to speak.) Anyway he always got into some kind of trouble because he liked to gamble and use heroin.

Those two "vices" will get you killed in prison. I helped him get out of a jam a few times over the years. Even on the streets. The last time I saw him we were in Soledad Prison in 1986. Not too long ago, he finally got out of the Feds after doing about fourteen years for bank robberies.

Anyway, back to the story. CRC in 1973 was a recruiting ground for a couple of Mexican prison gangs. It seemed like everybody I knew from my hometown was joining up. One old friend of mine talked to me about joining. I knew him most of my life and did time in CYA with him. He "ran it down to me" (explained) the purpose and reasons for the gang and some of the rules.

Now all gangs have rules. Whether street gangs or prison gangs. It doesn't take a rocket scientist to figure out that a criminal, like myself, likes to break the rules. If I remember right, one of their rules was that you can't use heroin. That left me out. I told him with all due respect that they would probably try to kill me because I liked using heroin and I knew I couldn't stop. And that was the truth!

Needless to say, I knew quite a few guys that got involved and regretted their decision later on in life. Note: Every one of us is just "one bad decision away" from ruining our life. All it takes is one decision. After you make it, everything starts going downhill pretty fast.

CHAPTER 19

NOBODY CAN CHANGE ME

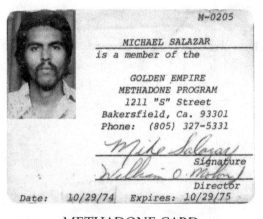

METHADONE CARD

I was released from CRC in 1974. Now I'm back in Bakersfield and have to check in with my new PO. I was a day late to report and he was pissed. So he sits there and tells me, "My name is—but they call me Baretta [like the old cop show] because I always get my man."

He was the kind of parole officer that would chase you and jump fences. Anyway, after his introduction, he asks me, "So what's your plan, Salazar?" (When you are released from prison, the state gives you $200 and that's it—$100 at the gate and a $100 when you check in with your parole officer. I think it's still like that.) I said to him, "You're going to give me my hundred dollars and I'm going to the connection and buy some heroin and fix [get high]. Then I'll use the rest to buy some more heroin and sell it so I can have some money in my pocket." Just telling him the truth.

Actually I didn't care what he thought. It didn't really matter. Nobody could change me, and to be honest, I didn't want to change. Bad attitude! So he laughs and tells me, "Well, at least you're honest." He said that everybody always says to him that they're going to find a job, straighten up their act, and not use drugs anymore. Usually a bunch of lies.

Anyway because I told him the truth he said that I have three dirty tests coming, which means that when he asks me to pee in the bottle and I know I'm giving him a "dirty test," on the third dirty test, I should go ahead and run (become a fugitive). Well, that was fine with me. At least we knew where we stood. Cop vs. criminal. But Baretta did tell me that the parole office knows everything that the parolees are doing because there are so many snitches that want to stay out, they tell them everything. It's worse today. Like I said, you will get told on sooner or later.

Oh well, went right back to using again. I did not understand my addiction. Never heard of an NA meeting. Started slinging that dope again, learning all the tricks to give my PO a clean test so I can stay out a little longer. Everybody was getting on Methadone in order to stay out. So did I.

The reason I got on the Methadone program was because of my PO (parole officer). I had already started running from parole (absconded, PO chasing you, etc.). He actually tried to help me and said that if I turned myself in, he would give me a thirty-day "dry out" (detox) at Tehachapi Prison and then put me in the Methadone program after I got out. I took a chance and he kept his word.

During those days there was only two yards in Tehachapi Prison, medium and minimum security. When I got to the medium yard, I didn't know anyone and I was dope sick. I ran into some old enemies that tried to threaten me. Make a long story short, I also ran into my little friend from YA (youth authority) that beat up Goliath. He and his friends helped me out and things got resolved. (Never know who you're going to meet in prison, huh?)

CHAPTER 20

ARE YOU PREPARED?

Me, my wife, and Big D

I tell that to all the youngsters that I talk to out here. I tell them the truth about prisons and drugs. Most of these "younsters" that are gangbanging (street gang affiliated) don't have a clue of what's going to happen to their life. Reminds me of a friend of mine named Big D.

He was a member of the Mexican Mafia but got saved in prison. (I was there in Soledad prison when he was preaching to the fellas.) Donald dedicated his life to reaching young people. One of his favorite sayings, when he talked to all those youngsters was "Are you prepared?"

Are you prepared to spend the rest of your life in prison? Are you prepared to spend years in a small little cell? Are you prepared to kill somebody? Are you prepared to be killed? Are you prepared to maybe turn gay? (No girls in prison, just "pitchers and catchers.") Are you prepared to never drive a car, go on a date, eat "menudo," be with your family, never have kids or if you do, have someone else raise them? Are you prepared to have Sancho (another guy) be with your woman?

Big D. was always real with everyone. He did not pull any punches. I miss that brother. He passed away a few months ago. I got a chance to visit him a couple of weeks before he went to be with the Lord. Even though he was sick, he was still going to the juvenile hall to talk to the youngsters there. Big D. never changed his style. God just changed his heart.

Anyway, the Methadone Maintenance Program is a government-sanctioned program designed to control your addiction. Methadone is supposed to take away your "craving" for heroin. It does, I guess, if you let it. I lasted about a year on it. Every morning you go to a "clinic" to get your dose. A little cup of liquid. After a while, your whole life revolves around your daily dose. Can't go anywhere without getting your dose. The problem is, is that every now and then you still want to use heroin and so you do. But it takes three times the amount to get you high. People have died because of that reality. Not only that, but "kicking methadone is ten times worse than kicking heroin."

Needless to say, I started selling heroin again while I was on the methadone maintenance program and one thing led to another. I started using again and now I had two bad habits. I was addicted to Methadone and heroin. Yup, I was in bad shape. Eventually, everything crashes down on you and so I was sent back to CRC on a violation. Here we go again.

CHAPTER 21

SLIPPING INTO DARKNESS
(GOING DEEPER AND DEEPER)

CCI TEHACHAPI

I transferred to Tehachapi Prison early in 1975 and my life took a turn for the worse.
Everything was just starting to jump off back then. Pure madness. Southern, Northern, Sureño, Norteño, Affiliated, Sympathizer, Neutral, Divided, La EME, Mafia, Nuestra Familia, AB (Aryan Brotherhood), BGF (Black Gorilla Family), Pegadas (Hits/Killings/

Stabbings), Lock it up, Peceta (PC protective custody), Lop, Lame with no game, Square from Delaware, Pimps, Players, part-time gangsters and Scandalous Vatos are words that describe the early seventies and eighties. Needless to say, it was almost impossible not to get involved. Especially if you were raised in that thug life.

Got involved with my old friends that were there again, and the rest is history. In the Mexican thug life, there are two sides. The Southern Mexicans and the Northern Mexicans. Southern California and Northern California, Bakersfield being the center of the state. In those days Bakersfield was a Norteño town. (That's the way it used to be. Nowadays, it's all changed. But back then, that's the way it was!) Needless to say, I made some decisions during this time that changed the course of my life. And I was not the only one.

We were all young back then. Young and dumb. I have pictures of the old crew back then. Some are dead, some are still in prison, a couple on death row, and the others are still hustling on the street, still using heroin or on methadone. It's sad when you think about it. Wasted years and wasted life. Our decisions always have consequences. Good or bad.

But back to the story. I caught a new case while I was there in Tehachapi and was sent to the "hole" (solitary confinement). Now I'm in real trouble. I was getting excluded from my N number and going to be re-sentenced on my original charges which was five to fifteen years in prison. Man, that was not good. Big D and a few others were in the hole at that time, but I will always remember one guy in particular. His name was Chuy. He was a jailhouse lawyer and taught me how to go "Pro Per" (how to defend myself in a court of law).

I explained my situation and so he ordered a couple of law books for me to study. He taught me how to file a writ of habeas corpus and the legal terminology such as, "Petitioner so states that pursuant to the following facts, etc., etc.," but most important he prepared me to face the judge in a courtroom and what to say and what to do. I really didn't think I could do it but I had no choice. I had no money, no attorney, and I knew that a public defender would be useless.

CHAPTER 22

ATTORNEY "PERRY MASON" AT YOUR SERVICE

So there I go back to Kern County Jail where I had a lot of enemies at the time. Big D had just come back from the Kern County Jail. He told me to be *thrucha* (be careful). [Where it started and how it all happened that I had enemies is a long story.]

Anyway, my day in court finally came and it was a packed courtroom. They called my name, read the charges, and asked me how I pled. I said, "Not guilty, Your Honor, and if it pleases the court, may I approach the bench?" He said yes and so I did. I said, "Your Honor, under the first, fifth, eighth amendment of the United States [can't remember anymore what amendments I actually quoted, but it was something like that], I am letting the court know that I'm going 'propria persona' pro per, i.e. [one who represents himself in a court of law]. I want a single cell with paper, pencils, and a typewriter and access to the law library. I want ten telephone calls a day so that I may prepare a proper defense. I want a legal investigator to investigate the charges filed against me. I want a legal clerk appointed to file every affidavit throughout my trial." I went on and on. I almost asked him for a coffee pot and the newspaper.

Man, that judge blew his top. He got so mad he turned beet red and began to yell at me in that packed courtroom. He said, "You guys that come from prison and think you are jailhouse lawyers, what makes you think you're qualified to defend yourself?" I said, "Your Honor, I have a high school diploma and two years of college." He yelled, "What college did you attend?" I said, "San Jose State College." He yelled, "What did you major in?" I said, "One year of pre-law and one year of psychology!" (I was lying…only went up to the eighth grade.)

He was angry and began to deny this and deny that and told the bailiff to take me away and put me in segregation so I could think about what I'm doing. The last thing I said was, "Your Honor, I would like the record to show that I am filing a writ of habeas corpus." And that's that. Anyway, I gave it my best shot.

Just before my preliminary hearing date, an assistant district attorney came to see me. He read the writ of habeas corpus that I was filing and told me, "Not bad for an amateur." I said, "Yeah, I know, but the court must do what I said they must do." He asked me, "What exactly do you want?" (Sounds like let's make a deal, huh?) I said, "How about six months in the county jail, credit for time served, no probation, no parole?" He just laughed and said, "With your record, that'll never happen." I said, "Well, make me an offer I can't refuse." He said, "How does this sound? We'll give you ten months in the county jail, no prison time, and no more parole. You will have one year probation running concurrent with your jail time so that when you get out, you will only have two months left on probation and that's it." Dang! That sounded good to me. No more prison or parole. And that's what happened. So there I go to Lerdo County Camp. A big shot lawyer now (smile) and what do I do? I escape!

CHAPTER 23

THE GREAT ESCAPE

Yup, I definitely did not like that road camp. I was there about a week when I made up my mind to escape. So one day we were out chopping weeds. There were seventeen guys in the crew. I had never been to road camp or done any county time, so I actually did not know where we were at. So I started asking the guys, as we were chopping weeds, if anyone wanted to escape with me. Everybody said no except this youngster who was doing ninety days.

He was just as crazy as I was. So I told him, "When you see me start the army truck, throw down your hoe and run to the truck." So pick up on this, there's seventeen guys chopping weeds (like in *Cool Hand Luke* movie), a Mexican cop that doesn't like Mexicans watching our every move, and the army truck behind him. So I ask Officer R—if I could sharpen my hoe. He mumbled something derogatory and said go ahead. (The sharpening tools were in the back of the truck).

So when I reached the truck, I stepped up on the rail and looked in. Yup, the keys were in the ignition. I went to the back of the truck and told the trustee to split (take off). This guy would drive the truck up little by little for the cop as we slave laborers made progress with the weeds. Anyway, the cop didn't see what I was doing because he's in front of the truck looking at the road crew. So I opened the door and got in. And immediately I realized that I didn't know how to drive this truck because it had two-compound gears. But it's too late now. I was in the truck.

All this time, the seventeen guys were looking at what I was doing while they're chopping weeds but the officer didn't know what's going on. Oh well, I stepped on the clutch, started the truck, and engaged the compound gears, hoping I get it right. I waved my hand looking at the youngster and said, "Come on!" So he dropped his hoe and ran past the cop to the truck and got in.

I told him, "Roll up the window and lock the door. Are you ready?" Yup he's ready! So I popped the clutch and took off on probably fourth-gear, jerking all the way up the road. The officer couldn't believe what was happening and jumped off the road as we went by. Youngster took off his shirt and rolled down the window and waved his shirt at all the fellas as we drove by. Man, that was funny when you think about it. Two Mexicans in a stolen army truck driving around that orchard looking for a way out to the main road. One didn't know how to drive the truck and the other one waving his shirt out the window like if he was in a parade. (Wish I had a camera.)

CHAPTER 24

HOW FAR CAN YOU RUN?

Don't ask me how we got away, but we did. Drove to Bakersfield the back way and ended up in the Loma neighborhood on Height St. Parked the truck, stole the toolbox, and went down the street to his sister's house. Caught a ride to my neighborhood and the rest is history. Our mug shots came out on TV that night so I knew we had to leave town, quick, fast, and in a hurry. Youngster went to LA and I went to Santa Ana with my family that lived in the Fifth St. neighborhood. Crazy neighborhood.

I ended up staying with my cousin Terri and her three daughters. They were young back then in 1976. I always remember that Terri used to send the girls to that little neighborhood church on Sunday and I would make fun of them all the time for going to church. I was not a believer at that time.

I remember when I was a kid, my grandmother asked me to take her little *santito* (statue) to the church in my neighborhood and get it blessed by the *padre* (Father). So I went to the rectory where they lived at and knocked on the door. The father opened the door holding a glass of wine in one hand and a cigarette in the other. He said, "What do you want?" I told him that my grandmother wanted him to bless her statue. He held out his hand and said that would cost me five dollars. This was like 1961 or 1962 so that was a lot of money. I told him that I didn't have any money so he just shut the door in my face. I think it was right there that I turned against religion. I got angry and went to the church and got the holy water and did it myself. My grandma never knew what happened.

Anyway, back to Orange County. I didn't stay too long because I didn't have any money and I never liked being a leech or being a *pidichi* (always begging or asking for a handout), so I went back to Bakersfield. Needless to say, I started selling heroin again because, in reality, it's all I knew how to do. I knew the cops were looking for me so I moved around from motel to motel always trying to be one step ahead of the Narcs (narcotics detectives).

As a matter of fact, years later I found out that they used to call me "the ghost" because every time they would get a tip of where I was at, when they kicked the doors in, I was gone. Back in the days, they had the HIP squad, Heroin Impact Program probation officers, taking all the junkies off the streets.

Years later one of them worked at the drug court and used to tell this pretty girl that worked there stories about a guy they called the ghost and how he escaped from Lerdo Road Camp. That pretty girl ended up being my wife.

Just in case you're reading this book and you think you want to make a career of being a drug dealer or just a criminal, remember this…you will get told on. Someone will snitch you off. They'll call 1-800-Drop A Dime. That's an old saying because back in the days, it would cost ten cents to make a phone call to the cops.

Anyway, back to the story. So finally, I got caught. (What else is new?) The total time that I stood out was about six weeks. That's about it. But now I have all kinds of charges against me. Including escape.

I defended myself again and made a deal for two to ten years. And there I go to Chino Guidance Center with a new prison number B# 79193.

CHAPTER 25

SUSANVILLE PRISON B#79193

Got to the guidance center with a couple of other guys from Bakers (Bakersfield). It was rough back then for Chicanos from Bakersfield because of the gang situation. In the seventies, Bakers was predominantly a "Northern/Nuestra Familia town. So the guidance center in Chino was EME territory. So it doesn't take a rocket scientist to figure out that there were a lot of problems for guys coming from Bakersfield.

So I was housed in "Stick a More" (Sycamore unit). It was a nickname that everyone understood. A lot of guys got "stuck" or stabbed in there.

Anyway, I ended up going up north to Susanville prison early in 1976. A million miles from nowhere. The prison was so far up in Northern California that we were lucky to get a letter. Only a few things I remember about Susanville. One, I almost had to kill someone because of a debt that wasn't mine. Two, I learned to fix copy machines. Three, I started a riot in which the national guard had to come, pulled us out in the snow half naked, and sent two busloads of us to San Quentin and Folsom in the middle of the night.

I learned a couple of good lessons in Susanville. Lesson #1 some guys say they're somebody when they're not. A guy I knew from Bakers, but not too well, owed some money to people on that prison yard. He was transferring to another prison but was waiting on the *clavo* (drugs) to come in. He asked me to get the drugs and pay off his debt and keep the rest. I agreed only *if* the drugs came in and I said that in front of the guys that he owed the money to.

Anyway, you probably know the story. He takes off and the drugs never come. Now I'm the only guy from Bakers (Bakersfield) on the yard and everybody knows it. So these guys approach me and tell me that I owe that debt. I said, "No, I don't." They said, "Yes, you do." I said, "No, I don't. Remember the conversation? No drugs, no money to be paid."

They didn't care. I owed them now and that was that. So they turned around and walked away. So a few days later, this youngster Marcos from Bakers arrived. I didn't know him but I knew his brothers on the street. A couple of days later he came to me and asked me if I had a problem on the yard. I hadn't told anybody about anything. He said that a friend of his that worked in the laundry told him that he pulled out the stash of "shanks" (knives) for the so-called "shot callers" (guys that control the yard) to use on me. At the same time some friends in my dorm asked me what was going on.

Apparently those guys were telling everybody in their yard what was going to happen to me. I got mad, so I decided to deal with this issue the way I was taught (face to face). So I got a knife, told the youngster to be my "point man" (look out), went to Sierra yard, and gathered those three guys together and told them, "I'm not paying you nothing. I don't owe you nothing, and if you don't like that, then let's go to dorm 26 and settle it. I got my "stuff" so go get yours and let's settle this now."

I actually don't remember what they said to me, but basically everything was squashed right there. Turns out, they weren't who they said they were. Lesson #2, when you start a riot, not everybody will show up. (How I got involved and ended up starting that riot is another story.) Anyway, once the riot started and the cops started "busting caps" (shooting), things changed for the worst. National Guard showed up, escorted us outside in the snow to the classification building, and held a kangaroo court.

One by one they interviewed us and asked us what we knew and where were we at. I told them that I was watching TV in the dayroom and that I personally didn't mess around or get involved with riots. They didn't believe me. Threw us in the hole and sent us out in the middle of the night. Some to San Quentin and some to Folsom. I was on the Quentin bus.

CHAPTER 26

SAN QUENTIN PRISON

San Quentin Prison. East Block Yard Side. Ugly-looking prison. I learned a lot in there about prison politics, the power of prison gangs, and the true insanity of prison life. The funny thing is that I actually liked doing time in that prison if you had to do time. Some of us that came down from the riot went to the Max-B yard and some to the mainline. That was me.

That was a crazy world in there. People walked around insane, wearing raincoats in the summertime. Everybody dodged the seagulls so they don't poop on you. The "Goon Squad" (cops) beat up convicts. Convicts beat up the "gooners." Guys got slapped, stabbed, or killed for different reasons. Boxing matches were in the sky lite gym. I still have the San Quentin newspaper for December 1977. Interesting articles.

A guy I knew from Susanville prison was attacked with a hatchet. Almost lost his arm. And I heard that the guy that attacked him had to PC (go into protective custody) because he did a sloppy job. I think everybody was a little bit nuts in there. Even myself.

But my cellie kept me sane. He was the funniest comedian I knew. He was better than George Lopez and Chris Rock put together. We laughed from morning to night. He was illiterate so I used to write his letters for him. The best letter to get a package sent went like this. "My darling, my wonderful one, I will always be grateful for the things that you've done. I smiled when you kissed me and I thrilled at your touch. My only sin is I love you much too much." Yup, a thirty-pound package on the way!

One day when all the Mexicans were locked down in their cells, a guard came to my cell and told me to roll it up because I was going home. I didn't believe it. I wanted to see some paperwork. But yup, it was true. SB 42 law had passed and was kicking out a lot of convicts. I just happened to be one of them.

Glad to get out of there. At the gate, they give you $100 and that's it. You have to find your own ride, which I did.

CHAPTER 27

THE BAKERSFIELD INN

Back in Bakersfield. Nothing's changed. Selling dope. Everybody's robbing and stealing. I was out about ninety days when I caught a Under the Influence/Paraphernalia charge. Did a ninety-day sentence. I was innocent on this one. I happened to be at friend's house when they raided the pad. Oh well. A few years later, a lawyer told me, "Mike, if you didn't have bad luck, you wouldn't have no luck at all!" Sounds about right so far.

So sometime in 1979, I was staying in a room at the Bakersfield Inn (before it closed down). This friend of mine rented the room so I could cut and bag the heroin. It was midnight when he took off to go pick up my girlfriend at the bar where she worked at. But they were taking too long. I felt something was wrong, so I gather up everything, drugs and balloons, etc., and put them in a paper sack and went outside.

Outside is a hallway that's pitch black. No one could see me. As I got close to the parking lot, I saw a couple of Narcs crouching behind some cars. They didn't see me so I threw the bag away from me underneath a car. They didn't see me do it. Right at that time another Narc finally saw me and drew his gun, placed me under arrest, and took me back to the room.

Now how did they know what room I came out of? We just rented the room a couple of hours before. Naturally somebody told. Anyway, they tossed the room and found the guns but no dope. So they started looking outside and finally found the bag. They came back in and said, "Look what we found." But I never saw that bag before in my life! They couldn't prove it. I knew the law. The room was not registered in my name so they couldn't pin me on the guns and that bag was not in my possession. I could beat this case blindfolded in a court of law! Wrong!

The police report said that officer saw me in the hallway with the bag in my hand and that he told me to set the bag down next to my feet. That put the bag of drugs in my possession. Lies. But who do you think the jury will believe? Me or a cop? Oh well, let's make a deal time again, and there I go on the "Goose" (prison bus) one more time, again!

CHAPTER 28

WHOSOEVER SHALL CALL UPON THE NAME OF THE LORD SHALL BE SAVED

Well, I made a deal for two to ten years again. Actually, it was sixteen months to two to three years and my low points sent me to Tehachapi prison. Been here before. This prison was like a country club. Golf (9 holes), gym, etc. So I go right back to my old routine—handball, dominoes, pinochle, hanging out with the fellas, drinking coffee, lying and telling "war stories." Same o, same o!

I was in dorm 7. An eighty-man dorm. One day I made ten gallons of "pruno" wine and kept it in my locker. On the fourth day we broke it out in the evening. Man, it was strong. We all got drunk and thought we were in a night club, walking up and down the dorm with a tumbler of wine in our hands. Needless to say we got busted and went to the hole.

The next day was March 1, 1980. A day I will always remember.

That morning I woke up with a mean hangover. The officer told me that I got a visit. Well, I wasn't expecting anyone so I tell him to go away. But he was *terco* (stubborn). He kept insisting that I go to this visit. So I end up going. Back in those days, if you were in the hole, they let you visit for twenty minutes if your charges were minor. So there I go cuffed and wearing these funny-looking "pixie shoes" to the visiting room.

These two ladies were sitting there that I didn't know. (I saw them a few years before in the county jail. They would come in on Sundays and sing in the cell blocks and talk to the inmates. Most of us would just cover our heads with a blanket and act like we were asleep. Didn't want to hear it. Just telling the truth!)

So I sat down and said to myself, "Who are these people and what do they want?" Sister Ethel told me, "Mike, the Lord told us to come visit you." The what? The who? I had never been to church and I definitely didn't know the Lord personally. I was sent to a Catholic church when I was young and even made my First Communion and Confirmation but I didn't really understand what that all meant. It was just something you were supposed to do. Never understood the church service because it was in Latin.

Actually I did go to a Pentecostal church service when I was on methadone in the early seventies. My counselor was a Christian and kept bugging me to go to church with him. So finally I said yes. That night I went with him to church. It was quite an experience. I stood out like a sore thumb. Everybody was wearing a suit. The women wore long dresses and had a doily or something on their head. I was wearing a Pendleton shirt and Levi's. So anyway, the service is jumping. The band and congas were playing, and everyone was running around in circles. The preacher was yelling and saying, "The power of God is in the house" and he would point to people and they would fall down. Some would come up to the stage and he would touch their head and they would fall. A whole bunch of people. I saw two guys I knew from the neighborhood that had become Christians and they fell. Man, I didn't know what was going on. Like I said, I had never been to church. So all of a sudden the preacher said, "There's a brother in the church today that needs Jesus." And he pointed to me and said, "Come on up, brother." Man, I didn't want to go. But he kept pointing, so there I go. He told me, "Do you believe in the Lord?" I said, "I guess so." He slapped me on my forehead like he did to the others and nothing happened. I didn't fall! So he told me again if I believed in the Lord and I said, "I guess so" and he slapped my forehead again. Nothing! I didn't fall. So he started pumping up the people and got ready to slap me the third time. I knew that if I didn't fall, I would be up there all night until I did. So when he asked me again and touched my forehead I fell to one knee. Yup, I was faking it. (Years later I found out it's called a CD "courtesy drop" when you fake falling down.) I didn't know what else to do to get out of there. I got up real slow and acted like I was stunned and went back to my seat. Needless to say I was glad to get out of there.

CHAPTER 29

THIS POOR MAN CRIED AND THE LORD HEARD HIM

Sister Ethel and Virgie

So here I was in front of these "holy roller ladies" that I really didn't know. This was thirty-five years ago, so the only thing I remember was that they told me that Jesus loved me! To be honest, I was cold inside. Those words didn't mean anything to me. I told them the truth. I didn't believe in Jesus and love was not in my vocabulary. What does love mean? Who knows.

I didn't grow up with hugs and kisses and encouraging words. My family was cold. I didn't grow up like "Leave It To Beaver" or "Father Knows Best" or like the "Cosby Family" or the "Brady Bunch." That's all make believe, not reality. And if there is a God, so what? He ain't never done nothing for me. That was my attitude.

I actually believed in the Von Daniken theory. That an intelligent life force came to earth and experimented with the monkeys and genetically altered us into humans. That was better than believing in evolution…that somehow, after billions of years, an amoeba was created and that became a fish, and the fish crawled on land and became an animal and that evolved into a bird, etc. Now that's stupid. Von Daniken theory is more believable.

Anyway, I was being honest to those ladies. I told them that I respected them for coming to visit me but I just didn't believe all that. So now visiting was over and Ethel and Virgie asked me if they could pray for me before they leave. I said yea, I guess so. (I actually thought they were going to pull out the rosary and pray. I never had anyone really pray for me.)

So one grabbed my left hand and the other my right hand and began to shout out loud, right there in the visiting room, "Lord in the Name of Jesus, we claim this soul for the kingdom of God. And devil, we command you to loosen your grip upon this man and command you to leave him. He's going to serve God no matter what! Amen!" And then they left. Man, was I embarrassed. Right there in front of everybody! Man, I couldn't wait to get back to the hole.

CHAPTER 30

SOMETHING HAPPENED

After I was in my cell for about an hour, something began to happen to me. In my mind I began to "see" Mike Salazar. The real Mike without the mask. All the wasted years that I have lived, all the people that I have hurt in one way or another. All the ugly things about myself that I made it a point to never look at. It was as if I was looking at a movie in my mind that I couldn't stop. (A man that does time in prison must learn to control his mind and turn things off. If not, he'll go crazy.)

So somehow I'm being forced to look at myself. And the more I see, the uglier it gets. I struggled now within myself. I didn't know what's going on. I didn't understand that something or someone was chipping at the ice in my heart. I looked up and somehow in this emotional state that I'm experiencing I challenged God by blurting out, "Si Tu Eres Dios [If you're God, the Supreme Being, the Creator, Infinite Intelligence, or whatever they call you], then change my stinking life. Right here, right now. Not tomorrow, or next week but right now because I don't believe anything!"

And I meant what I said. I wasn't playing games, or trying to get out early or get my ol' lady back, etc. Nothing like that. I was sincere and meant what I said with all my heart!

Right at that moment, I felt a rush come over my body. It was like as if someone poured a cold bucket of water on me. But it started at my feet and travelled upward to my head. And when the rush reached my head, a dam full of tears broke.

I instantly knew *He was God and that I was a sinner.* (I actually knew somehow what sin meant even though those two ladies never mentioned anything like that to me). Every sin that I committed in my life flashed before my "eyes" one at a time (layer by layer was being peeled off like an onion). It started when I was a kid, and after every sin that was revealed to me, I wept like a baby. I'm talking "boo-hoos." I realized what I had done and was sorry for the things that I had done and wept with all my heart.

As soon as I wept and meant it, I began to laugh because it felt so good. And then the next sin would "appear" in my mind and I would weep bitterly for what I had done. After I was done weeping, then I would start laughing. Weeping for my sins and laughing because I felt His forgiveness. Crying and laughing. Crying and laughing! This went on for hours. I was so full of dirt inside!

I woke up the next day kind of confused. "Did that really happen to me?" I wondered. I never read the Bible, so I really didn't understand what happened to me. I didn't know that I was Born Again. I never read that "Whosoever shall call upon the name of the Lord shall be saved." I didn't know anything so I kind of put my experience in a cabinet of my mind and closed the door. No one knows what happened. Just me. And that's what I did till I was released back on the main line.

CHAPTER 31

RAISE YOUR HAND

Choose you this day whom you will serve

—Joshua 24:15

When I went back to the yard, I didn't tell anyone what had happened to me. So I just went back to my old prison routine. In prison, when you're playing dominoes or handball or cards, everybody "caps" or "talks smack" and "clowns" each other (cuss, makes fun of each other, and calls each other names but in a joking way).

But something had changed. Something was wrong. I found myself angry and frustrated and couldn't take a joke anymore. I took everything personal. So my friends didn't even want me around them and I didn't want or care to be either. I went to the gym and beat up that heavy bag every day trying to release this frustration inside me. I was one miserable guy. I thought maybe I was just burned out with dormitory living and needed to transfer to another prison that has cells. I really didn't understand what was going on with me. This went on for about two weeks.

But one night I was up writing a letter about midnight when all of a sudden the Lord spoke to me. It was my voice but it wasn't my voice, a thought, an impression, whatever, but this is what He said, "Do you see how miserable you are? Well, it's going to get worse unless you make up your mind and come to me!" Now I instantly knew what He was talking about. God wanted me to make a commitment. To "raise my hand" and dedicate my life to Him.

I understood commitment. All gang members, convicts, and criminals understand that. If you *raise your hand* and say you're going to do something, then you have to do it. Otherwise, don't raise your hand.

Well, the first thing I said was, "Hey God, how can I make a commitment to you if I'm the way I am? I refuse to be a hypocrite, especially in here. Nobody likes a fake, phony or a fraud, and I'm not like that. Anyway, how can I be a Cristiano [Christian] if I still like getting high, I like getting drunk, I like women and porn [I had Miss March playboy pinned up in my locker]. I like the fast life, the money, and even all the drama and chaos that I live in every day in prison and on the street. So how can I make that kind of commitment to you if I'm this way?"

Well, needless to say, I thought I talked my way out of that but He had an answer for my questions. He said, "So what? So what if you're that way? You can't change yourself, can you? You just make up your mind to serve Me and I will change you!" Man, I couldn't get out of that one.

I tried to change before. I read psychology books like *I'm OK, You're OK...the Power of Positive Thinking*. I tried working, I tried methadone, I tried everything that I knew of, to maybe change, but nothing worked or lasted for me. I actually stopped trying to change a long time ago. So I made up my mind to serve God and once again the Holy Spirit bathed me with His presence (just like in the hole) and I wept before God once again.

CHAPTER 32

FLY YOUR COLORS, ESE!

The next day I found a small "Convicts for Christ" Bible and began to read. It was amazing. The Word of God was alive to me and it made sense. I kept the Bible hidden for a while and would read every morning when I walked the track. (I was an undercover closet Christian for a bit.) But one day I read a scripture that said, "If you're ashamed of Me, I'll be ashamed of you." Dang, I wish I wouldn't have read that. I knew instantly what He meant. "Fly your colors, Ese!".

In other words, I needed to let everyone know that I was a Christian. If I had the courage to go to any prison or jail that I was sent to and let it be known where I stood and who I was affiliated with and to also be that way on the streets, then why not let it be known who you're with now?

Easier said than done. I'm new at this and the fear of what others will say or do is a powerful obstacle. But a man has to overcome that fear and do what God says he should do. So I was obedient. From that day on, things in my life really changed. I placed a "big" Bible right on top of my locker in plain sight of everyone. I forced myself to carry that big Bible everywhere I went.

The first time it felt like it was burning in my hand and that everyone was looking at me. And they probably were. But nobody said anything. Actually, when I made that commitment with God that night, I had one condition. I told the Lord that if anyone said something to me, I was going to have to get down or fight. Remember, I'm new at this.

So now I started going to the chapel and in time started telling everybody on the yard about Jesus.

Man, I was on fire. I told everybody. Cops, inmates, homeboys, prison personnel. I even talked to the birds and the ants on the track (smile). People didn't know what was going on with me. It got to where the inmates would avoid me because they knew I was going to talk to them about the Lord. It was funny.

In the mornings when I would walk the track, some of the gang would approach me and walk with me. They would say, "Mike, what's wrong with you, ese? Why are you going to the chapel and picking up that Bible? You're not weak, you're not a punk, you're not doing a lot of time. You're like one of us! What's going on?" And so I would "witness" to them and tell them what happened to me in the hole and about my commitment to God and about Jesus this and Jesus that…Jesus, Jesus, Jesus. Yeah, they would last one time around the track but they all said the same thing. They said, "If I ever go that way, I got to be real!" My response was always, "That's the only way you can be is Real!" They knew I wasn't faking it. I thank God for the mercy and courage that He gave me during that time.

CHAPTER 33

GET ON YOUR KNEES

I began to understand what it really meant to be a Christian in prison because I didn't know how to be one yet on the street. Prison was my training ground. It was like being in boot camp learning the basics. Listen, learn, and obey! That's the key to change.

The Bible says to forgive others so I wrote to my sister Evelyn and asked her to forgive me. We hadn't talked in a few years. She was mad at me for causing my mom to get sick from worry, which was true. But when you're out there doing your thing, you never admit to anything. Always in denial. So I wrote her and told her about Jesus. Jesus this and Jesus that. Jesus, Jesus, Jesus. Well, she called my mom and told her, "Mom, you better go and visit Mickey [my childhood name] because he 'done flipped his lid.' He went crazy. Maybe all that LSD and Mescaline he took finally caught up with him." It's funny because her son, my nephew Steve, was on the same yard with me and witnessed my transformation. Years later he got saved and served the Lord on the street before he passed away a couple of years ago.

So here comes my mom with my dad. They had to come and see if I "went crazy" or not. At our visit, I came out with my little Bible and told them what happened to me. If anyone knows you, it's your family.

So my dad asked me, in private, what he should do with the guns he was holding for me. He knew I would never get rid of them just like that. I think he was testing me to see if I was for real. I told him to sell the guns or get rid of them because I don't want them anymore. That's not my life anymore. That's where my dad knew I was not playing games. If you become a Christian, you will be tested to see if you mean what you say and to see if you've really changed.

About two months have gone by and I'm going through major changes and learning a lot. One day I'm sitting on my bunk and brother Fidel is passing by and says to pray for him because he was taking a test at school. (I used to call him Billy Goat because he had a long beard.) He was fifty-two years old and I was twenty-nine. We used to argue about everything. He asked me why did God save me at twenty-nine and wait so long to save him?

My answer was that God loved me more than him! I was always joking with him but I would make him mad. Fidel is the one that taught me to play the guitar.

Anyway, my way of praying up until this time was to sit on my bunk and bow my head. Well, I started to pray when I heard distinctly, "Get on your knees." (Actually, the command interrupted my thoughts.) Man, what was that? Oh well, I started again when I heard, "Get on your knees" the second time. Dang, that scared me. So in order not to hear anything, I began to whistle.

Whistling was my old way of trying not to be scared. When we were kids we used to walk through the Union cemetery at midnight when we would come from parties on the other side of town so that the cops wouldn't bust us for curfew violation. It's quiet, dark, and spooky in the cemetery, so all the Mexican stories that my grandmother told me about would be going through my mind, e.g., the "llorona" (the lady that wandered around crying looking for her kids that she killed) or the "Lechusa" (the owl that was really a witch… you can hear them all the time around my neighborhood). She would say, "Mijo, when you hear that witch flying by, make sure you cuss her out!" I definitely did that. Superstitions can have a powerful grip on you.

So I'm whistling to myself when I hear it again the third time, "Get on your knees." And baam, just like that, I get on my knees because I realized it was the Lord talking to me. As I'm kneeling, I'm laughing because I understood why I was supposed to kneel. He was humbling me and shaving off a little bit of pride that I was full of and to see if I was going to do what He's telling me to do. So from that time on, I prayed on my knees in that eighty-man dorm.

After a while, a funny thing started to happen. When guys would come in the dorm blasting their boom box (radio), they would turn it down when they passed by my bunk if I was on my knees praying. *I think it was a matter of respect for God.*

CHAPTER 34

CLAP YOUR HANDS

For whom the Son has Set Free is Free Indeed

—John 8:36

When I started going to the chapel, I couldn't clap my hands. I wanted to, but I couldn't. It seemed like everybody could clap to the music but I didn't know how, if that makes any sense. I was still hard inside and it seemed like I had steel cables wrapped all around me. I couldn't move. I asked the Lord plenty of times to help me clap but nothing happened. Finally, the Lord told me, "Just do it!" So I forced myself to clap. One clap at a time. It took a while, but finally it got easier for me. Now lifting my hands up in the air was another story but I forced myself on that one too. One hand at a time.

Pretty soon, I was even tapping my feet (smile). God was "breaking chains" in my life that needed to be broken so that I could be *free* to worship Him the way he wanted me to. I understood what He was doing but most of the time I didn't like it.

Now one of the things Chaplain Jonas would say at the beginning of the service was, "Go and shake somebody's hand." Well, this big black brother who was about six feet eight inches would come to me and "bear hug" me. Now I had never hugged a man before so I was like in shock. I didn't know how to act. It was awkward to say the least. Man, this guy hugged me every time I went to the chapel. I found myself sitting way in the back just so he wouldn't see me, but sure enough, that guy would look for me and bear hug me!

I couldn't hug him back. I knew I should, but I couldn't. So I forced myself. I remember that day he approached me to give me a hug. Well, I beat him to the punch and gave him a bear hug. *I felt the chains drop off.* It got easier as time went on.

One day the chaplain says that there was going to be a foot washing service.

Well, as far as I was concerned, I was *not* going to wash anybody's feet—white feet, black feet, or Mexican feet. Forget about it! It ain't happening. I struggled with this issue all week. The reality was that I was still prejudiced.

Everybody in prison is prejudiced. Whites with whites, blacks with blacks, Mexicans with Mexicans. Man, I didn't even trust or like some of my own race let alone wash their feet. Nobody in his right mind would wash another race's feet. Especially in prison. Uh-uh. Not me! But Jesus washed His men's feet and He was God. So why can't we? It doesn't matter. I'm not washing feet! End of story!

Well, needless to say, when they released everyone to the chapel that one night, I found myself being forced to go. The Holy Spirit is the teacher. You're either going to do what he says or you're not. Obey Him or not! *But I was committed. I had to!* So there I go, dragging my feet. But I went.

Once inside the chapel, the guys started singing and somebody read John chapter 13. I don't remember who washed my feet first, but I felt the chains drop off. And yes, I washed feet too! It's amazing what obedience can do for a man.

CHAPTER 35

OBEDIENCE IS BETTER THAN SACRIFICE
"JUST GIVE IT TO HIM"

I lived in dorm number 7. Everybody was calling it the "Christian dorm" because there were about ten of us serving the Lord in there. One day a brother in Christ came by and said he was collecting things to give to the new Christian brothers that just drove up (arrived). Like a care package.

So I went to my locker to see what I had to spare. I got an envelope, a bar of soap, and I had two tubes of toothpaste. One was new and one was half-empty. So I naturally grabbed the half a tube and started to walk down the aisle toward the front door when I heard Him say, "What are you doing?" Well, I knew immediately what He was talking about. God wanted me to give up the new tube, not the half! But I said, "Now wait a minute, God, I don't even know this dude, and anyway, he will be glad to receive a half a tube. It's better than none! That guy should be grateful."

Well, what can I say? I had to go back to my locker and get the full tube of toothpaste and give it away and so I kept the half! I definitely wasn't very happy about this scenario. Until I realized what He was trying to teach me. *Always try and give your best!* Always give your best. That's a lesson I have learned over and over throughout the years.

I remember I gave away my one and only Pendleton shirt to a guy that was going home. He was no one in particular. Just someone that God wanted me to give my shirt to. That's all.

One other example of obedience for me was traumatic. I was in the dorm. Everybody knew I was a Christian and everybody on the yard knew too. Well, this guy came up to me and asked me for a "fix" of coffee (a scoop of instant coffee). So I said no problem. I had enough left. A little while later, the same guy came back and asked me for another fix of coffee. Well, my first response to him was going to be, "Dude you better go spread your hustle." In other words go beg somewhere else because there ain't no punks here." (That was my old prison mentality surfacing in this situation. In prison you can't let anyone take advantage of you because you would be considered weak.)

It seemed to me he was trying to "play me" (take advantage) because he knew I was a Christian. But before I could say anything I heard, "Just give it to him! Give it to him!" So I went back into my locker and put the scoop in a paper and handed it to him. Man, it took everything in me to be obedient, I thought.

Well, a little while later here comes the same guy and asked me for another fix. Man, that's it. I knew that he thought I was some kind of punk or something. "You better get on down the ramp tramp" was formulating in my mouth when I heard again, "Just give it to him!" Dang! Didn't want to hear that but either you're going to obey or you're not regardless of how you feel about it or what anyone else might say.

So I did, grudgingly, knowing that this dude was taking my kindness for weakness, knowing that he might brag to his friends of what he did, knowing that I would never have allowed this to happen in the past, knowing that it went against my grain to give in like that, and feeling like a chump by giving it to him. But like I said, I did it.

After he walked away, I understood what God was doing in me. Breaking my pride and my old prison mindset that was ingrained in me all these years. The Bible says, "Humble thyself in the sight of the Lord and He will lift you up!" But it doesn't feel good.

I learned something that day that has helped me for years after. Obedience to God is not determined by how you feel or by some emotion. It's determined by your commitment. If you raised your hand then do it. Simple as that!

There were so many lessons that I was learning. So many changes that I was going through. One after another after another. It was confusing to me. Is this what everyone goes through?

Well, the answer came one day while I was walking the track. I heard "Tiny Bubbles." Tiny bubbles? What does that mean? I knew already just to be quiet and listen. He said, "You are like a glass of water with bubbles in it. The bubbles always surface then burst and disappear. The bubbles inside of you are all your hang ups, character defects, stinking thinking, wrong attitudes, and weaknesses that need to be changed. But they have to surface so you can see them. Once you see them, then you will know what to pray for and then you will have the victory over them!"

Made sense. You never know you have a problem until you "see" it. I was blind but now I see!

CHAPTER 36

STEAK AND CHERRY PIE

Well, it's Thursday night. Me, Benny, and Gary are going to the chow hall. On the menu are steak and cherry pie. Everybody went that night. The only bad thing about this meal is that you always leave the chow hall hungry. You never get seconds.

I had been reading Mark 11.22–24: "If you speak to this mountain and tell it to move and don't doubt in your heart, it will happen. Therefore, whatever you desire, believe that you have received it and you will get it." So before we get to the chow hall I talk to Benny and Gary. I said, "Do you believe what this scripture says?" They said, "I guess so!" They weren't sure. But neither was I. I had never seen God move before. Never had an actual prayer answered that was visible. Actually, I've only been "saved" about two months and Benny and Gary about a month. (I led Benny to the Lord.) All three of us are "babes in Christ." The funny thing is that I'm trying to teach them and I don't even know what I'm doing.

So here we go. My explanation of this verse. The Bible says that (1) if you have a desire (we're hungry and we never get seconds) (2) speak to the mountain and tell it to move (be specific), (3) don't doubt, and (4) believe that you have received it already (so thank Him for it as if you already have it).

So all three of us came in agreement and prayed "Lord, we're hungry. So we want extra steak and cherry pie [specific]." Then we thanked Him because what do you say when somebody gives you something? Thank you!

CHAPTER 37

DOUBT IS OUR ENEMY

As soon as we prayed and got in line the battle was on. I'm talking about a fight in my mind. The conversation went something like this. "Man, what's wrong with you? You know you're not supposed to ask for things like that! That's not right! That prayer will never be answered! God doesn't answer prayers like that fool."

No! No! No! The word of God says whatever we desire when we pray, believe that we receive and we'll get it! I had a mean ol' conversation going on. It's not going to happen! Yes, it is! No, it's not! Yes, it is! You're wrong! No, I'm not! Man, talk about schizophrenic! If you would have heard my mind on a loud speaker, you definitely would have said, "Surely Big Mike has lost his mind!"

So the "battle" is raging as we get to the tray rack. I put my tray on the line (the food line consists of a bunch of convicts serving each dish). Immediately, this dude comes from the back and gives me an extra pie. (I didn't even know this guy.) I look back at Benny and Gary and they have the same look on their face as I know I did.

Scary! Something was going on and it was kind of spooky. So we three Musketeers sit down, bow our heads, and say grace in the middle of about two to three hundred convicts. Now remember. This is prison. White boys eat with white boys, blacks with blacks, and Mexicans with Mexicans. That's just the way it is in there. But when you raise your hand and let it be known that you're a Christian in prison, you can't allow the race thing to rule your life.

You see, Gary was white and an ex-Satan worshipper. He's got a cold testimony. Apparently he was a warlock and ruled a coven of witches. His initiation involved letting a demon that looked like a goat/man possess him. Now that's scary! I didn't mess around like that. When we were kids, me and my cousin played the Ouija board one time and it talked to us. No doubt, that was the last time I played that thing. Like I said, Gary was a white boy and Benny was a "pimpin' Will from Sugar Hill" Chicano from San Diego. I used this term to describe any person who thinks he's a ladies' man or player. (The saying goes, Pimpin Will from sugar hill, never worked and never will, get your hand shook and your money took. Just don't call me late for dinner.) He was also the barber in the prison.

CHAPTER 38

HERE COMES THE STEAK

So here we are the Three Musketeers. After we say grace, we were talking about this extra pie that I got, when a "pinto" (convict) yelled at me from one side of the chow hall and said, "Hey, Mike, you want some more steak?"

Man, I got up, went over to him, said *gracias* (thank you), and came back to my table. As soon as I sat down, another guy yelled at me from another side of the chow hall, "Hey, Mike, you want some more steak?" I got up, went over to him, told him *gracias*, and came back to my table. (In case you're wondering why these guys are yelling, have you ever eaten with three hundred guys that are all talking at the same time in one room? Noisy!) Anyway, I just sat down the second time when once again someone else yelled at me, "Hey, Mike, want some more steak?" I got up, went over to him, said *gracias*, and came back to my table.

My God, I couldn't believe it. Three steaks. One for each of us! Talk about ecstatic! Nooobody gives away their steak. Noooobody!

CHAPTER 39

HERE COMES THE PIE

Then, just as we were in the middle of talking with our mouths full, here comes a guy, dressed in white (cook uniform) with a humongous pie tray full of cherry pie. He's coming from the back and dodging every table.

You see, all the guys were yelling at him, saying, "Over here, homes [homeboy]. Over here!" Everybody wanted some of that good ol' cherry pie.

But guess where he's coming to? Yup! Right to our table! It was like he made a beeline right to us. Then he said the magic words *Pongale* (Chicano slang for "go for it, dude!") So I went for it and scraped half the pie tray onto all three of our trays.

Now remember. A prison pie tray was about two feet wide and three feet long. So imagine three small mountains of cherry pie. One for each of us. We had so much food. Did we pig out? Yes! Did we lick the tray clean? Almost! What a miracle. We walked out of the chow hall that night full! What happened to us really was a miracle to say the least.

Thoughts to Ponder

It's funny sometimes who God uses to answer your prayers. God used three gangsters to answer our prayer. They were *not* Christians. And the "pie guy"? Never saw him before in my life. We didn't know him. So how in the world could he just go across the whole chow hall, right to our table, and "kick down" (give) all that pie to complete strangers? You tell me!

Ephesians 3:20: "Now unto him that is able to do exceeding abundantly above all that we could ask or think" describes what happened. God answered our prayer. We exercised a little faith and refused to doubt and God worked a miracle for us. It worked! I still approach the Lord in the same way thirty-five years later and it still works!

CHAPTER 40

IN RETROSPECT

As I sit here reliving this story of my life that I'm writing to you about, I realize just how good the Lord is. I'll be sixty-five years old in September. I've been out of prison now for twenty-seven years. I have a great relationship with my children, grandchildren, and great-grandchildren. I have a beautiful wife Angelina that loves the Lord. I am a blessed man.

I've been the Pastor of Set Free Ministries here in Bakersfield for twenty-three years and the founder of the Set Free Training Center (discipleship homes for men) for the last twenty-five years. I can go on and on and say with all humility, "Look what the Lord has done!" *And if he can do it for me, He can do it for you.* That's my hope. That's my prayer. That's my purpose for writing this book. All you have to do is tell Him what I told Him thirty-five years ago: *"If you're for real, God, then change my life!"*

Contact Info:
    Pastor Mike Salazar
    P.O. Box 3324
    Bakersfield, Ca. 93385

    www.setfreebakersfield.com
    Facebook: SetFree Bakersfield

CPSIA information can be obtained
at www.ICGtesting.com
Printed in the USA
FSHW011550240221
78885FS